50 French Pastry Dishes for Home

By: Kelly Johnson

Table of Contents

- Croissants
- Éclairs
- Madeleines
- Tarte Tatin
- Mille-Feuille
- Macarons
- Chaussons aux Pommes
- Pain au Chocolat
- Frangipane Tart
- Paris-Brest
- Galette des Rois
- Clafoutis
- Canelés
- Financiers
- Quiche Lorraine
- Tarte aux Fruits
- Parisian Cream Puffs
- Profiteroles
- Kouign-Amann
- Palmier
- Gâteau Basque
- Savarin
- Brioche
- Opera Cake
- Sablé Cookies
- Baked Camembert with Puff Pastry
- Breton Galette
- Chouquettes
- Nougatine
- Bûche de Noël
- Chocolate Tarte
- Choux Pastry with Crème Patissière
- Pot de Crème
- Poached Pears in Puff Pastry
- Vanilla Bean Soufflé

- Tarte au Citron
- Pistachio Croissants
- Fig and Almond Tarts
- Hazelnut Praline Cake
- Saint-Honoré Cake
- Fruit Clafoutis
- Palmiers with Chocolate
- Cherry Frangipane Tart
- Lemon Meringue Pie
- Orange Blossom Madeleines
- Raspberry Tartelette
- Pear and Almond Puff Pastry
- Coffee Éclairs
- Apricot Jam Puff Pastries
- Rustic Apple Galette

Croissants

Ingredients:

- 2 1/4 teaspoons active dry yeast
- 1/2 cup warm milk
- 1/4 cup sugar
- 3 1/2 cups all-purpose flour
- 1 teaspoon salt
- 3 tablespoons unsalted butter, melted
- 1 cup cold unsalted butter (for lamination)
- 1/4 cup water
- 1 egg (for egg wash)

Instructions:

1. **Activate the Yeast:**
    - In a small bowl, dissolve the yeast and sugar in warm milk. Let sit for 5 minutes until foamy.
2. **Prepare the Dough:**
    - In a large bowl, mix flour and salt. Add the yeast mixture and melted butter. Stir until combined. Add water slowly until a dough forms.
3. **Knead:**
    - Knead the dough for 5-7 minutes until smooth. Cover and refrigerate for 1 hour.
4. **Laminate the Dough:**
    - Roll out dough into a large rectangle. Place cold butter between two sheets of parchment paper and roll it into a flat rectangle. Place butter in the center of the dough and fold the edges over to encase the butter. Roll out and fold into thirds. Refrigerate for 30 minutes. Repeat this process 3 times.
5. **Shape and Proof:**
    - Roll dough into a large rectangle and cut into triangles. Roll each triangle tightly into a croissant shape. Let them proof for 2 hours.
6. **Bake:**
    - Preheat the oven to 400°F (200°C). Brush the croissants with an egg wash and bake for 15-20 minutes until golden brown.

Éclairs

Ingredients:

- 1 cup water
- 1/2 cup unsalted butter
- 1 cup all-purpose flour
- 4 large eggs
- 1/4 teaspoon salt
- 1/2 teaspoon vanilla extract

For the filling:

- 2 cups heavy cream
- 2 tablespoons powdered sugar
- 1 teaspoon vanilla extract

For the glaze:

- 4 oz dark chocolate
- 1/4 cup heavy cream

Instructions:

1. **Make the Choux Pastry:**
    - Preheat the oven to 425°F (220°C). In a saucepan, bring water and butter to a boil. Stir in flour and salt. Cook for 1-2 minutes. Remove from heat and cool slightly.
2. **Add Eggs:**
    - Add eggs one at a time, mixing until smooth after each addition. Stir in vanilla extract.
3. **Pipe and Bake:**
    - Pipe the dough into 4-inch long strips on a baking sheet. Bake for 20-25 minutes until golden and puffed. Let cool.
4. **Make the Filling:**
    - Whip the cream, powdered sugar, and vanilla extract until stiff peaks form. Pipe into the cooled éclairs.
5. **Make the Glaze:**
    - Heat the heavy cream until simmering, then pour over chopped chocolate. Stir until smooth. Dip the tops of the éclairs into the chocolate glaze and let set.

Madeleines

Ingredients:

- 1/2 cup unsalted butter, melted
- 3/4 cup all-purpose flour
- 1/2 teaspoon baking powder
- Pinch of salt
- 1/2 cup granulated sugar
- 2 large eggs
- 1 teaspoon vanilla extract
- Zest of 1 lemon
- Powdered sugar (for dusting)

Instructions:

1. **Prepare the Pan:**
   - Preheat the oven to 375°F (190°C). Grease and flour madeleine pans.
2. **Mix the Batter:**
   - In a bowl, whisk flour, baking powder, and salt. In a separate bowl, beat eggs and sugar until light and fluffy. Stir in vanilla and lemon zest.
3. **Combine:**
   - Fold in the dry ingredients, then add melted butter. Spoon the batter into the prepared pans.
4. **Bake:**
   - Bake for 10-12 minutes until golden and springy to the touch. Let cool slightly before removing from the pans.
5. **Serve:**
   - Dust with powdered sugar and serve.

Tarte Tatin

Ingredients:

- 6-8 medium apples (Granny Smith or Golden Delicious)
- 1/2 cup unsalted butter
- 1 cup granulated sugar
- 1 sheet puff pastry
- 1 teaspoon vanilla extract
- 1 tablespoon lemon juice

Instructions:

1. **Prepare the Apples:**
    - Peel, core, and halve the apples. Squeeze lemon juice over them to prevent browning.
2. **Caramelize:**
    - In a skillet, melt butter over medium heat. Add sugar and cook until it turns a golden caramel color. Add the apples and cook for 10-12 minutes until they soften.
3. **Assemble:**
    - Preheat the oven to 375°F (190°C). Place a round baking dish over the apples. Roll out the puff pastry and place it over the apples, tucking in the edges.
4. **Bake:**
    - Bake for 25-30 minutes until the pastry is golden and puffed.
5. **Invert and Serve:**
    - Let the tart cool slightly before carefully inverting it onto a plate.

Mille-Feuille

Ingredients:

- 1 package puff pastry
- 2 cups heavy cream
- 1/4 cup granulated sugar
- 1 teaspoon vanilla extract
- 1 tablespoon cornstarch
- Powdered sugar (for dusting)

Instructions:

1. **Prepare the Puff Pastry:**
    - Preheat the oven to 400°F (200°C). Roll out the puff pastry and cut into 3 long strips. Bake for 15-20 minutes until golden and crisp.
2. **Make the Pastry Cream:**
    - In a saucepan, heat the cream until just simmering. In a bowl, whisk together sugar, cornstarch, and vanilla. Slowly pour the hot cream into the mixture while whisking. Return to the saucepan and cook until thickened. Let cool.
3. **Assemble:**
    - Layer the puff pastry with pastry cream between each layer.
4. **Serve:**
    - Dust the top layer with powdered sugar before serving.

Macarons

Ingredients:

- 1 cup powdered sugar
- 1 cup almond flour
- 3 large egg whites
- 1/4 cup granulated sugar
- 1/4 teaspoon cream of tartar
- Food coloring (optional)

For the filling:

- 1/2 cup unsalted butter, softened
- 1 cup powdered sugar
- 1 teaspoon vanilla extract

Instructions:

1. **Prepare the Shells:**
    - Preheat the oven to 300°F (150°C). Sift almond flour and powdered sugar together. In a separate bowl, beat egg whites with cream of tartar until soft peaks form. Gradually add granulated sugar and continue to beat until stiff peaks form. Fold in the dry ingredients and food coloring.
2. **Pipe the Macarons:**
    - Pipe the batter onto a lined baking sheet in small circles. Let them sit for 30 minutes to form a skin.
3. **Bake:**
    - Bake for 15-20 minutes until set. Let them cool completely.
4. **Make the Filling:**
    - Beat butter, powdered sugar, and vanilla until smooth. Pipe onto one macaron shell and sandwich with another.

Chaussons aux Pommes

Ingredients:

- 1 sheet puff pastry
- 2 apples, peeled and chopped
- 1/4 cup sugar
- 1 tablespoon butter
- 1/2 teaspoon cinnamon
- 1 egg (for egg wash)

Instructions:

1. **Make the Apple Filling:**
    - Cook apples with sugar, butter, and cinnamon in a pan until tender, about 10 minutes. Let cool.
2. **Assemble the Chaussons:**
    - Preheat the oven to 375°F (190°C). Cut puff pastry into squares. Place a spoonful of the apple mixture in the center, fold over, and seal the edges.
3. **Bake:**
    - Brush with egg wash and bake for 15-20 minutes until golden brown.

Pain au Chocolat

Ingredients:

- 1 sheet puff pastry
- 4 oz dark chocolate, chopped
- 1 egg (for egg wash)

Instructions:

1. **Assemble:**
    - Preheat the oven to 400°F (200°C). Cut puff pastry into rectangles. Place a piece of chocolate in the center and fold the pastry over.
2. **Bake:**
    - Brush with egg wash and bake for 15-20 minutes until puffed and golden.

Frangipane Tart

Ingredients:

- 1 tart shell, baked
- 1/2 cup almond flour
- 1/2 cup unsalted butter, softened
- 1/2 cup powdered sugar
- 2 eggs
- 1/4 teaspoon vanilla extract
- 1 tablespoon all-purpose flour

Instructions:

1. **Make the Frangipane:**
    - Preheat the oven to 350°F (175°C). Cream butter and sugar together. Add eggs, one at a time, followed by almond flour, vanilla, and flour. Mix until smooth.
2. **Assemble:**
    - Fill the baked tart shell with frangipane and bake for 25-30 minutes until golden.

Paris-Brest

Ingredients:

For the Choux Pastry:

- 1 cup water
- 1/2 cup unsalted butter
- 1 cup all-purpose flour
- 1 teaspoon granulated sugar
- 1/4 teaspoon salt
- 4 large eggs

For the Praline Cream Filling:

- 1/2 cup hazelnuts, toasted and finely chopped
- 1/2 cup sugar
- 1 cup heavy cream
- 1/2 cup milk
- 3 large egg yolks
- 1/4 cup cornstarch
- 1 teaspoon vanilla extract

Instructions:

1. **Make the Choux Pastry:**
    - Preheat the oven to 375°F (190°C). In a saucepan, bring water and butter to a boil. Stir in flour, sugar, and salt. Cook for 1-2 minutes until the dough pulls away from the sides of the pan.
    - Remove from heat and beat in eggs, one at a time, until smooth and glossy.
2. **Pipe and Bake:**
    - Pipe the dough into a ring on a parchment-lined baking sheet. Bake for 30-35 minutes until golden and puffed. Let cool.
3. **Make the Praline Cream:**
    - In a saucepan, combine sugar and hazelnuts. Cook until golden and caramelized. Add cream and milk, heating to a simmer. In a separate bowl, whisk egg yolks and cornstarch. Slowly whisk in the hot milk mixture. Cook until thickened. Stir in vanilla extract and let cool.
4. **Assemble:**

- Cut the choux pastry ring in half. Fill with praline cream and top with the other half. Dust with powdered sugar and serve.

Galette des Rois

Ingredients:

- 2 sheets puff pastry
- 1 cup almond flour
- 1/2 cup unsalted butter, softened
- 1/2 cup powdered sugar
- 1 large egg
- 1 teaspoon vanilla extract
- 1 tablespoon dark rum
- 1 egg yolk (for egg wash)

Instructions:

1. **Make the Almond Filling:**
   - In a bowl, combine almond flour, softened butter, powdered sugar, egg, vanilla, and rum. Mix until smooth.
2. **Assemble:**
   - Preheat the oven to 375°F (190°C). Roll out puff pastry and place one sheet on a baking sheet. Spread the almond filling on top, leaving a small border. Place a feve (small figurine) in the filling. Place the second pastry sheet on top and press the edges to seal.
3. **Egg Wash:**
   - Brush the top with egg yolk and score the surface with a knife.
4. **Bake:**
   - Bake for 25-30 minutes until golden brown and puffed. Let cool slightly before serving.

Clafoutis

Ingredients:

- 2 cups pitted cherries (or other fruit like plums or apricots)
- 1/2 cup all-purpose flour
- 1/2 cup granulated sugar
- 1/4 teaspoon salt
- 3 large eggs
- 1 cup whole milk
- 1 teaspoon vanilla extract
- Powdered sugar (for dusting)

Instructions:

1. **Prepare the Fruit:**
   - Preheat the oven to 350°F (175°C). Grease a baking dish and arrange the pitted cherries evenly.
2. **Make the Batter:**
   - In a bowl, whisk together flour, sugar, and salt. Add eggs, milk, and vanilla. Whisk until smooth.
3. **Bake:**
   - Pour the batter over the cherries and bake for 35-40 minutes, until puffed and golden. Dust with powdered sugar before serving.

Canelés

Ingredients:

- 1 cup whole milk
- 1/2 cup unsalted butter
- 1 vanilla bean (or 1 teaspoon vanilla extract)
- 1 cup all-purpose flour
- 1/2 cup granulated sugar
- 2 large eggs
- 1 tablespoon dark rum
- 1 tablespoon vanilla extract

Instructions:

1. **Make the Batter:**
    - Preheat the oven to 425°F (220°C). In a saucepan, heat milk, butter, and vanilla until simmering. Remove from heat and let cool.
2. **Combine Ingredients:**
    - In a bowl, whisk together flour, sugar, and eggs. Add the cooled milk mixture, rum, and vanilla. Mix until smooth.
3. **Bake:**
    - Pour the batter into canelé molds and bake for 45 minutes to 1 hour, until dark and caramelized on the outside. Let cool slightly before unmolding.

Financiers

Ingredients:

- 1/2 cup unsalted butter
- 1/2 cup almond flour
- 1/2 cup powdered sugar
- 1/4 cup all-purpose flour
- 4 large egg whites
- 1/4 teaspoon vanilla extract
- Pinch of salt

Instructions:

1. **Prepare the Butter:**
    - Preheat the oven to 375°F (190°C). Melt butter in a saucepan until golden brown, then let cool.
2. **Make the Batter:**
    - In a bowl, whisk together almond flour, powdered sugar, flour, and salt. Add egg whites and vanilla. Stir in melted butter.
3. **Bake:**
    - Spoon the batter into financier molds and bake for 12-15 minutes until golden. Let cool before serving.

Quiche Lorraine

Ingredients:

- 1 pie crust, pre-baked
- 6 slices bacon, chopped
- 1/2 cup grated Gruyère cheese
- 1/2 cup heavy cream
- 1/2 cup whole milk
- 4 large eggs
- Salt and pepper to taste
- 1/4 teaspoon nutmeg

Instructions:

1. **Cook the Bacon:**
   - Preheat the oven to 375°F (190°C). Cook bacon in a skillet until crispy. Remove and drain on paper towels.
2. **Make the Custard:**
   - In a bowl, whisk together eggs, cream, milk, salt, pepper, and nutmeg.
3. **Assemble:**
   - Spread bacon and grated Gruyère in the pre-baked pie crust. Pour the custard mixture over it.
4. **Bake:**
   - Bake for 30-35 minutes until set and golden. Let cool before serving.

Tarte aux Fruits

Ingredients:

- 1 pre-baked tart shell
- 1 cup pastry cream (see recipe for the crème pâtissière)
- Assorted fresh fruits (such as berries, kiwi, apples, and peaches)
- Apricot glaze or melted jelly (for brushing)

Instructions:

1. **Make the Pastry Cream:**
    - Prepare a batch of pastry cream by cooking milk, sugar, and eggs to thicken, then let cool.
2. **Assemble the Tart:**
    - Spread the cooled pastry cream into the pre-baked tart shell. Arrange the fruit on top in a decorative pattern.
3. **Glaze:**
    - Brush the fruit with apricot glaze or melted jelly to give it a shiny finish.
4. **Serve:**
    - Refrigerate the tart until ready to serve.

Parisian Cream Puffs (Choux à la Crème)

Ingredients:

- 1 cup water
- 1/2 cup unsalted butter
- 1 cup all-purpose flour
- 1 teaspoon sugar
- 4 large eggs

For the cream filling:

- 2 cups heavy cream
- 1/2 cup powdered sugar
- 1 teaspoon vanilla extract

Instructions:

1. **Make the Choux Pastry:**
    - Preheat the oven to 400°F (200°C). In a saucepan, bring water and butter to a boil. Stir in flour and sugar. Cook until the dough forms a ball. Remove from heat and beat in eggs, one at a time.
2. **Pipe and Bake:**
    - Pipe small mounds of dough onto a baking sheet. Bake for 20-25 minutes until golden. Let cool.
3. **Make the Cream:**
    - Whip heavy cream with powdered sugar and vanilla until stiff peaks form. Pipe the cream into the cooled puffs.
4. **Serve:**
    - Dust with powdered sugar and serve.

Profiteroles

Ingredients:

- 1 cup water
- 1/2 cup unsalted butter
- 1 cup all-purpose flour
- 1 teaspoon sugar
- 4 large eggs

For the filling:

- 2 cups whipped cream or vanilla ice cream

For the chocolate sauce:

- 4 oz dark chocolate
- 1/4 cup heavy cream

Instructions:

1. **Make the Choux Pastry:**
    - Preheat the oven to 400°F (200°C). In a saucepan, bring water and butter to a boil. Stir in flour and sugar. Cook until the dough forms a ball. Remove from heat and beat in eggs, one at a time.
2. **Pipe and Bake:**
    - Pipe small mounds of dough onto a baking sheet. Bake for 20-25 minutes until golden. Let cool.
3. **Fill the Profiteroles:**
    - Once cooled, fill the puffs with whipped cream or ice cream.
4. **Make the Chocolate Sauce:**
    - Heat the cream in a saucepan. Pour over chopped chocolate and stir until smooth.
5. **Serve:**
    - Drizzle chocolate sauce over the profiteroles before serving.

Kouign-Amann

Ingredients:

- 2 1/2 cups all-purpose flour
- 1/2 cup warm water
- 1 packet active dry yeast
- 1/2 cup unsalted butter, softened
- 1/2 cup sugar
- 1/2 teaspoon salt
- 1/4 cup additional butter, melted

Instructions:

1. Make the Dough:
    - In a bowl, combine warm water, yeast, and a pinch of sugar. Let sit for 5 minutes until bubbly. Add flour, salt, and the rest of the sugar, mixing into a dough. Knead until smooth.
2. Rest the Dough:
    - Let the dough rise for 1 hour in a warm place until doubled in size.
3. Roll and Fold:
    - Roll the dough into a rectangle. Spread softened butter on the dough and sprinkle with sugar. Fold the dough into thirds, then roll it out again. Repeat folding and rolling 3 more times.
4. Shape and Bake:
    - Roll dough into a round shape and place in a buttered pan. Let rise for 30 minutes. Bake at 375°F (190°C) for 40-45 minutes, until golden and caramelized.

Palmier

Ingredients:

- 1 sheet puff pastry
- 1/2 cup granulated sugar
- 1 tablespoon ground cinnamon (optional)

Instructions:

1. Prepare the Puff Pastry:
    - Preheat the oven to 400°F (200°C). Roll out the puff pastry sheet on a floured surface.
2. Sugar the Pastry:
    - Sprinkle sugar evenly on top. Optionally, add cinnamon.
3. Fold and Slice:
    - Fold each side of the pastry towards the center. Then, fold again from both sides to form a log. Slice into 1/2-inch pieces.
4. Bake:
    - Place the slices on a baking sheet. Bake for 12-15 minutes until golden and crisp.

Gâteau Basque

Ingredients:

- 1 1/2 cups all-purpose flour
- 1 teaspoon baking powder
- 1/2 teaspoon salt
- 1/2 cup unsalted butter, softened
- 1/2 cup granulated sugar
- 1 egg
- 1 teaspoon vanilla extract
- 1/4 cup almond flour
- 1/2 cup pastry cream (or cherry jam for traditional)

Instructions:

1. Make the Dough:
    - Preheat the oven to 350°F (175°C). In a bowl, combine flour, baking powder, and salt. In another bowl, cream butter and sugar. Add egg, vanilla, and almond flour, then mix in the dry ingredients until a dough forms.
2. Assemble the Cake:
    - Divide the dough in half. Press half into the bottom of a greased cake pan. Spread pastry cream or cherry jam over the dough. Top with the remaining dough, smoothing the surface.
3. Bake:
    - Bake for 35-40 minutes until golden. Let cool before serving.

Savarin

Ingredients:

- 1/2 cup warm milk
- 1 tablespoon active dry yeast
- 3 eggs
- 2 1/2 cups all-purpose flour
- 1/2 teaspoon salt
- 1/4 cup sugar
- 1/4 cup unsalted butter, melted
- 1/2 cup dark rum
- 1 cup heavy syrup or fruit juice (for soaking)

Instructions:

1. Prepare the Dough:
    - In a bowl, combine warm milk and yeast. Let it bubble. Add flour, sugar, salt, eggs, and butter. Mix until a sticky dough forms.
2. Rise and Bake:
    - Let the dough rise for 1 hour. Then shape it into a ring in a greased savarin mold. Bake at 375°F (190°C) for 30-35 minutes until golden.
3. Soak:
    - Once baked, soak the savarin in syrup or rum and juice mixture until fully absorbed.

Brioche

Ingredients:

- 1/2 cup warm milk
- 2 teaspoons active dry yeast
- 1/4 cup sugar
- 3 1/2 cups all-purpose flour
- 1/2 teaspoon salt
- 4 large eggs
- 1 cup unsalted butter, softened

Instructions:

1. Activate the Yeast:
    - In a bowl, dissolve yeast and sugar in warm milk. Let sit for 5 minutes until bubbly.
2. Make the Dough:
    - Add flour and salt to the yeast mixture. Mix in eggs, one at a time, and knead until dough is smooth. Gradually incorporate butter.
3. Rise and Bake:
    - Let dough rise for 1-2 hours. Then shape it into a loaf or small buns. Let it rise again for 1 hour. Bake at 350°F (175°C) for 25-30 minutes.

Opera Cake

Ingredients:

For the Coffee Syrup:

- 1/2 cup brewed coffee
- 1/4 cup sugar

For the Almond Sponge:

- 1/2 cup almond flour
- 1/2 cup all-purpose flour
- 5 eggs
- 1/2 cup sugar

For the Coffee Buttercream:

- 1/2 cup unsalted butter, softened
- 1 cup powdered sugar
- 2 tablespoons coffee

For the Chocolate Ganache:

- 1 cup dark chocolate
- 1/2 cup heavy cream

Instructions:

1. Make the Coffee Syrup:
    - Combine coffee and sugar in a saucepan, simmer until thickened.
2. Bake the Sponge:
    - Preheat the oven to 350°F (175°C). Beat eggs and sugar until fluffy. Fold in almond flour and all-purpose flour. Bake for 20 minutes, then cool.
3. Assemble the Cake:
    - Cut the sponge into thin layers. Brush with coffee syrup, layer with buttercream, and ganache. Repeat for multiple layers.
4. Finish:
    - Coat the top with ganache and refrigerate to set.

Sablé Cookies

Ingredients:

- 1 1/2 cups all-purpose flour
- 1/2 cup powdered sugar
- 1/4 teaspoon salt
- 1/2 cup unsalted butter, chilled and cut into pieces
- 1 teaspoon vanilla extract
- 1 egg yolk

Instructions:

1. Make the Dough:
    - Combine flour, sugar, and salt in a bowl. Cut in butter until the mixture resembles breadcrumbs. Add vanilla and egg yolk and knead until smooth.
2. Chill and Shape:
    - Chill the dough for 30 minutes. Roll out and cut into shapes.
3. Bake:
    - Preheat the oven to 350°F (175°C). Bake cookies for 10-12 minutes until lightly golden.

Baked Camembert with Puff Pastry

Ingredients:

- 1 wheel Camembert cheese
- 1 sheet puff pastry
- 1 egg, beaten (for egg wash)
- Fresh thyme (optional)

Instructions:

1. Prepare the Camembert:
    - Preheat the oven to 400°F (200°C). Unwrap the Camembert and place it in the center of the puff pastry.
2. Wrap the Cheese:
    - Fold the pastry around the cheese, sealing the edges. Brush with the egg wash and sprinkle with thyme.
3. Bake:
    - Bake for 20-25 minutes, until the pastry is golden brown. Let cool slightly before serving.

Breton Galette

Ingredients:

- 2 cups all-purpose flour
- 1/2 cup granulated sugar
- 1/2 teaspoon salt
- 1/2 cup unsalted butter, cold and cubed
- 1/4 cup cold water
- 1 large egg yolk
- 1 teaspoon vanilla extract
- 1 tablespoon rum (optional)
- 1 egg (for egg wash)

Instructions:

1. Prepare the Dough:
    - In a food processor, combine flour, sugar, and salt. Add butter and pulse until the mixture resembles coarse crumbs. Add water, egg yolk, and vanilla, pulse until dough forms.
2. Chill the Dough:
    - Wrap the dough in plastic wrap and refrigerate for at least 30 minutes.
3. Shape and Bake:
    - Roll the dough into a circle and transfer to a tart pan. Press it into the edges and refrigerate for 15 minutes. Brush with egg wash and bake at 350°F (175°C) for 25-30 minutes, until golden.

Chouquettes

Ingredients:

- 1/2 cup water
- 1/2 cup unsalted butter
- 1 cup all-purpose flour
- 1/4 teaspoon salt
- 4 large eggs
- 1/4 cup pearl sugar (for topping)

Instructions:

1. Prepare the Dough:
    - Preheat oven to 400°F (200°C). In a saucepan, combine water and butter. Bring to a boil, then remove from heat and stir in flour and salt. Return to heat and stir until the dough pulls away from the sides of the pan.
2. Add Eggs:
    - Add eggs one at a time, stirring well after each addition until smooth.
3. Shape and Bake:
    - Spoon dough into small mounds on a parchment-lined baking sheet. Sprinkle with pearl sugar. Bake for 20-25 minutes, until puffed and golden.

Nougatine

Ingredients:

- 1 cup granulated sugar
- 1/2 cup slivered almonds
- 2 tablespoons unsalted butter

Instructions:

1. Caramelize the Sugar:
    - In a pan over medium heat, melt the sugar until it turns golden brown. Stir in the butter until smooth.
2. Add Almonds:
    - Quickly add the almonds and stir to coat them in the caramel.
3. Cool and Shape:
    - Pour the mixture onto a parchment-lined baking sheet. Let it cool completely, then break into pieces.

Bûche de Noël (Yule Log)

Ingredients:

For the Sponge Cake:

- 4 large eggs
- 1 cup granulated sugar
- 1 teaspoon vanilla extract
- 1/2 cup all-purpose flour
- 1/4 cup unsweetened cocoa powder
- 1 teaspoon baking powder
- Pinch of salt

For the Buttercream:

- 1/2 cup unsalted butter, softened
- 1 cup powdered sugar
- 1/4 cup unsweetened cocoa powder
- 1 teaspoon vanilla extract
- 2 tablespoons milk

Instructions:

1. Make the Cake:
   - Preheat oven to 350°F (175°C). Beat eggs and sugar until fluffy. Sift together flour, cocoa powder, baking powder, and salt. Gently fold into the egg mixture. Pour into a lined baking pan and bake for 12-15 minutes.
2. Roll the Cake:
   - Once the cake is done, let it cool slightly, then roll it up with parchment paper. Let cool completely.
3. Prepare Buttercream:
   - Beat butter and powdered sugar until smooth. Add cocoa powder, vanilla, and milk to make the frosting.
4. Assemble the Log:
   - Unroll the cooled cake, spread with buttercream, and roll it back up. Frost the outside and decorate with chocolate shavings or powdered sugar.

Chocolate Tarte

Ingredients:

- 1 pre-baked tart shell
- 1 cup heavy cream
- 8 oz dark chocolate, chopped
- 2 tablespoons unsalted butter
- 1 teaspoon vanilla extract

Instructions:

1. **Make the Ganache:**
    - Heat the cream until it just starts to simmer. Pour over the chopped chocolate and let sit for 2 minutes. Stir until smooth, then add butter and vanilla.
2. **Fill the Tart:**
    - Pour the ganache into the pre-baked tart shell. Let set at room temperature for 1-2 hours before serving.

Choux Pastry with Crème Patissière

Ingredients:

For the Choux Pastry:

- 1/2 cup water
- 1/2 cup unsalted butter
- 1 cup all-purpose flour
- 1/4 teaspoon salt
- 4 large eggs

For the Crème Patissière:

- 1 cup whole milk
- 1/2 cup granulated sugar
- 4 large egg yolks
- 2 tablespoons cornstarch
- 2 teaspoons vanilla extract

Instructions:

1. **Make the Choux Pastry:**
   - Preheat the oven to 375°F (190°C). In a pan, bring water and butter to a boil. Stir in flour and salt until it forms a ball. Add eggs one at a time, mixing well.
2. **Bake the Choux:**
   - Spoon dough onto a parchment-lined baking sheet and bake for 20-25 minutes until puffed and golden. Let cool.
3. **Make Crème Patissière:**
   - Heat milk and sugar in a pan. Whisk together egg yolks and cornstarch, then pour in the hot milk mixture. Return to the heat and cook until thickened. Stir in vanilla and cool.
4. **Fill the Choux:**
   - Once the choux have cooled, slice them open and fill with crème patissière.

Pot de Crème

Ingredients:

- 2 cups heavy cream
- 1 vanilla bean, split
- 1/2 cup granulated sugar
- 4 large egg yolks
- 1/4 teaspoon salt

Instructions:

1. **Heat the Cream:**
    - In a saucepan, heat the cream with the vanilla bean until it just starts to simmer.
2. **Whisk the Eggs:**
    - In a bowl, whisk together egg yolks, sugar, and salt. Slowly pour the hot cream into the eggs, whisking constantly.
3. **Bake:**
    - Pour the custard into ramekins and place them in a baking dish. Add hot water halfway up the sides of the ramekins. Bake at 300°F (150°C) for 30-40 minutes.

Poached Pears in Puff Pastry

Ingredients:

- 4 ripe pears, peeled and cored
- 1 cup red wine
- 1/2 cup sugar
- 1 sheet puff pastry
- 1 egg (for egg wash)

Instructions:

1. **Poach the Pears:**
   - In a saucepan, combine red wine and sugar. Bring to a simmer, then add pears. Poach for 20-25 minutes until tender. Let cool.
2. **Wrap the Pears:**
   - Roll out the puff pastry and cut into squares. Place a pear in the center of each square and wrap it up. Brush with egg wash.
3. **Bake:**
   - Bake at 375°F (190°C) for 25-30 minutes, until golden.

Vanilla Bean Soufflé

Ingredients:

- 1 vanilla bean, scraped
- 1/2 cup whole milk
- 4 large egg yolks
- 1/4 cup granulated sugar
- 1/4 cup all-purpose flour
- 4 large egg whites
- 1/4 teaspoon cream of tartar
- Powdered sugar (for dusting)

Instructions:

1. **Make the Custard:**
    - Heat milk with vanilla bean and seeds. Whisk egg yolks, sugar, and flour in a bowl. Gradually pour in the milk, whisking constantly. Cook over low heat until thickened.
2. **Whisk the Egg Whites:**
    - Beat egg whites with cream of tartar until stiff peaks form.
3. **Assemble and Bake:**
    - Fold egg whites into the custard mixture. Pour into buttered soufflé dishes. Bake at 375°F (190°C) for 12-15 minutes, until puffed and golden. Dust with powdered sugar before serving.

Tarte au Citron (Lemon Tart)

Ingredients:

For the Tart Crust:

- 1 1/4 cups all-purpose flour
- 1/4 cup powdered sugar
- 1/2 cup unsalted butter, cubed
- 1 egg yolk
- 2-3 tablespoons cold water

For the Lemon Filling:

- 1 1/2 cups heavy cream
- 3/4 cup granulated sugar
- 3 large eggs
- 3 large egg yolks
- 1/2 cup fresh lemon juice (about 3 lemons)
- Zest of 2 lemons

Instructions:

1. **Prepare the Crust:**
   - In a food processor, combine flour, powdered sugar, and butter. Pulse until crumbly. Add egg yolk and pulse until dough forms. Add cold water as needed. Press into a tart pan and refrigerate for 30 minutes. Preheat oven to 350°F (175°C) and bake for 15-20 minutes until golden.
2. **Make the Filling:**
   - In a saucepan, combine cream, sugar, and lemon zest. Heat over medium until warm. In a separate bowl, whisk eggs and egg yolks, then slowly pour in the hot cream mixture, whisking constantly. Add lemon juice and strain mixture into the tart shell.
3. **Bake:**
   - Bake the tart at 325°F (160°C) for 25-30 minutes, until the filling is set. Let cool before serving.

Pistachio Croissants

Ingredients:

- 1 sheet puff pastry
- 1/2 cup pistachio paste
- 1/4 cup powdered sugar
- 1 tablespoon heavy cream
- 1 egg (for egg wash)
- 1/4 cup chopped pistachios (for garnish)

Instructions:

1. **Prepare the Filling:**
    - In a bowl, mix pistachio paste, powdered sugar, and heavy cream to form a smooth paste.
2. **Assemble the Croissants:**
    - Roll out puff pastry and cut into triangles. Place a spoonful of pistachio filling on the wide end of each triangle and roll up into croissant shapes. Brush with egg wash.
3. **Bake:**
    - Preheat the oven to 375°F (190°C). Bake for 15-20 minutes, until golden. Garnish with chopped pistachios.

Fig and Almond Tarts

Ingredients:

For the Tart Shell:

- 1 1/4 cups all-purpose flour
- 1/4 cup granulated sugar
- 1/2 cup unsalted butter, cubed
- 1 egg yolk
- 2 tablespoons cold water

For the Almond Filling:

- 1/2 cup almond meal
- 1/2 cup granulated sugar
- 1/4 cup unsalted butter, softened
- 2 tablespoons all-purpose flour
- 1 egg
- 1/2 teaspoon almond extract
- Fresh figs, sliced

Instructions:

1. **Make the Tart Shell:**
    - In a food processor, combine flour, sugar, and butter. Pulse until crumbly. Add egg yolk and water, pulse until dough forms. Refrigerate for 30 minutes, then roll out and press into tart pans. Bake at 350°F (175°C) for 15 minutes.
2. **Prepare the Almond Filling:**
    - In a bowl, mix almond meal, sugar, butter, flour, egg, and almond extract. Spread the almond mixture into the baked tart shells.
3. **Assemble the Tarts:**
    - Arrange fig slices on top of the almond filling. Bake at 350°F (175°C) for 20-25 minutes, until golden.

Hazelnut Praline Cake

Ingredients:

For the Cake:

- 1 cup all-purpose flour
- 1 cup ground hazelnuts
- 1 teaspoon baking powder
- 1/2 cup unsalted butter, softened
- 1 cup granulated sugar
- 3 large eggs
- 1 teaspoon vanilla extract
- 1/2 cup milk

For the Praline:

- 1/2 cup granulated sugar
- 1/4 cup chopped hazelnuts
- 2 tablespoons unsalted butter

Instructions:

1. **Prepare the Cake:**
   - Preheat oven to 350°F (175°C). Beat butter and sugar until fluffy. Add eggs one at a time, then add vanilla. Stir in flour, ground hazelnuts, and baking powder. Add milk and mix until smooth. Pour into a greased cake pan and bake for 30-35 minutes.
2. **Make the Praline:**
   - In a saucepan, melt sugar over medium heat until golden. Stir in butter and chopped hazelnuts, then pour over the cooled cake. Let set before serving.

Saint-Honoré Cake

Ingredients:

For the Puff Pastry:

- 1 sheet puff pastry

For the Choux Pastry:

- 1/2 cup water
- 1/2 cup unsalted butter
- 1 cup all-purpose flour
- 4 large eggs
- 1/4 teaspoon salt

For the Cream:

- 1 1/2 cups heavy cream
- 1/4 cup powdered sugar
- 1 teaspoon vanilla extract

For the Caramel:

- 1/2 cup granulated sugar

Instructions:

1. **Make the Puff Pastry:**
   - Roll out the puff pastry and cut into circles. Bake at 375°F (190°C) for 15-20 minutes.
2. **Make the Choux Pastry:**
   - Bring water and butter to a boil. Stir in flour and salt. Cook until the dough pulls away from the pan. Add eggs one at a time until smooth. Pipe small mounds onto a baking sheet and bake at 375°F (190°C) for 20 minutes.
3. **Whip the Cream:**
   - Beat the heavy cream, powdered sugar, and vanilla until stiff peaks form.
4. **Assemble the Cake:**
   - Pipe cream onto the baked puff pastry and choux puffs. Arrange them in a circle and drizzle with caramel.

Fruit Clafoutis

Ingredients:

- 2 cups mixed berries or stone fruit (cherries, peaches, etc.)
- 1/2 cup all-purpose flour
- 1/4 cup granulated sugar
- 1/2 teaspoon vanilla extract
- 3 large eggs
- 1 cup whole milk
- 1/4 teaspoon salt

Instructions:

1. **Prepare the Fruit:**
   - Preheat oven to 350°F (175°C). Arrange fruit in a buttered baking dish.
2. **Make the Batter:**
   - In a bowl, whisk together flour, sugar, eggs, milk, vanilla, and salt. Pour over the fruit.
3. **Bake:**
   - Bake for 30-35 minutes until golden and set. Serve warm or at room temperature.

Palmiers with Chocolate

Ingredients:

- 1 sheet puff pastry
- 1/2 cup granulated sugar
- 1/2 cup dark chocolate, melted

Instructions:

1. **Prepare the Puff Pastry:**
    - Sprinkle sugar on a clean surface. Roll out puff pastry and sprinkle with more sugar. Fold the edges towards the center, then fold again to form a log. Slice into pieces.
2. **Bake:**
    - Preheat oven to 375°F (190°C). Bake palmiers for 12-15 minutes until golden.
3. **Serve with Chocolate:**
    - Drizzle with melted chocolate before serving.

Cherry Frangipane Tart

Ingredients:

For the Tart Shell:

- 1 1/4 cups all-purpose flour
- 1/4 cup powdered sugar
- 1/2 cup unsalted butter, cubed
- 1 egg yolk
- 2 tablespoons cold water

For the Frangipane:

- 1/2 cup almond meal
- 1/4 cup granulated sugar
- 1/4 cup unsalted butter, softened
- 1 large egg
- 1 teaspoon vanilla extract

For the Filling:

- 1 1/2 cups fresh cherries, pitted

Instructions:

1. **Make the Tart Shell:**
    - Follow the instructions for the tart shell from the **Fig and Almond Tarts** recipe above.
2. **Prepare the Frangipane:**
    - Mix almond meal, sugar, butter, egg, and vanilla to form a smooth paste.
3. **Assemble the Tart:**
    - Spread frangipane in the baked tart shell. Arrange cherries on top. Bake at 350°F (175°C) for 30-35 minutes, until golden.

Lemon Meringue Pie

Ingredients:

For the Pie Crust:

- 1 1/4 cups all-purpose flour
- 1/2 cup unsalted butter, cubed
- 1/4 cup powdered sugar
- 1 egg yolk
- 2 tablespoons cold water

For the Lemon Filling:

- 1 1/2 cups granulated sugar
- 1/4 cup cornstarch
- 1 1/2 cups water
- 4 large egg yolks
- 1/2 cup fresh lemon juice
- Zest of 2 lemons
- 1 tablespoon unsalted butter

For the Meringue:

- 4 large egg whites
- 1/2 teaspoon cream of tartar
- 1/4 cup granulated sugar

Instructions:

1. **Make the Pie Crust:**
   - Follow the instructions for the tart shell from the **Fig and Almond Tarts** recipe above.
2. **Prepare the Lemon Filling:**
   - Combine sugar, cornstarch, and water in a saucepan. Cook over medium heat until thickened. Whisk in egg yolks, lemon juice, and zest. Stir in butter. Pour into the cooled pie crust.
3. **Make the Meringue:**
   - Beat egg whites and cream of tartar until stiff peaks form. Gradually add sugar and continue to beat until glossy.
4. **Assemble and Bake:**
   - Spread meringue over the lemon filling. Bake at 350°F (175°C) for 10-15 minutes until golden.

Orange Blossom Madeleines

Ingredients:

- 1/2 cup unsalted butter, melted and cooled
- 2/3 cup granulated sugar
- 2 large eggs
- 1 teaspoon vanilla extract
- 1 teaspoon orange blossom water
- 1 cup all-purpose flour
- 1/2 teaspoon baking powder
- Zest of 1 orange

Instructions:

1. **Prepare the Batter:**
   - Whisk eggs and sugar until pale and fluffy. Stir in vanilla extract and orange blossom water. Fold in flour, baking powder, and orange zest. Mix in melted butter.
2. **Chill:**
   - Cover the batter and refrigerate for 1 hour.
3. **Bake:**
   - Preheat oven to 375°F (190°C). Grease a madeleine pan, spoon batter into molds, and bake for 10-12 minutes until golden. Cool before serving.

Raspberry Tartelettes

Ingredients:

For the Tart Shells:

- 1 cup all-purpose flour
- 1/4 cup powdered sugar
- 1/2 cup unsalted butter, cubed
- 1 egg yolk
- 1-2 tablespoons cold water

For the Filling:

- 1/2 cup raspberry jam
- 1 1/2 cups fresh raspberries
- Powdered sugar (for dusting)

Instructions:

1. **Make the Tart Shells:**
    - Combine flour, sugar, and butter in a food processor until crumbly. Add egg yolk and water. Press into tartlet molds and bake at 350°F (175°C) for 12-15 minutes.
2. **Assemble the Tartelettes:**
    - Spread raspberry jam into each shell. Top with fresh raspberries and dust with powdered sugar.

Pear and Almond Puff Pastry

Ingredients:

- 1 sheet puff pastry
- 2 ripe pears, thinly sliced
- 1/4 cup almond meal
- 2 tablespoons granulated sugar
- 1/4 teaspoon cinnamon
- 1 egg (for egg wash)
- 1 tablespoon honey (for glazing)

Instructions:

1. **Prepare the Pastry:**
    - Roll out puff pastry and score a 1/2-inch border around the edges. Spread almond meal over the center.
2. **Add Pears:**
    - Arrange pear slices over the almond meal. Sprinkle with sugar and cinnamon. Brush edges with egg wash.
3. **Bake:**
    - Preheat oven to 375°F (190°C). Bake for 20-25 minutes until golden. Drizzle with honey before serving.

Coffee Éclairs

Ingredients:

For the Choux Pastry:

- 1/2 cup water
- 1/2 cup unsalted butter
- 1 cup all-purpose flour
- 4 large eggs
- 1/4 teaspoon salt

For the Coffee Cream:

- 1 cup heavy cream
- 2 tablespoons instant coffee granules
- 1/4 cup powdered sugar

For the Coffee Glaze:

- 1 cup powdered sugar
- 1 tablespoon brewed coffee

Instructions:

1. **Make the Choux Pastry:**
   - Bring water and butter to a boil. Stir in flour and salt, cook until dough pulls away. Add eggs one at a time until smooth. Pipe into éclairs and bake at 375°F (190°C) for 20 minutes.
2. **Prepare the Cream:**
   - Whip cream with coffee granules and powdered sugar until stiff. Fill éclairs with cream.
3. **Glaze the Éclairs:**
   - Mix powdered sugar with brewed coffee to make a glaze. Drizzle over éclairs.

Apricot Jam Puff Pastries

Ingredients:

- 1 sheet puff pastry
- 1/2 cup apricot jam
- 1/4 cup sliced almonds
- 1 egg (for egg wash)

Instructions:

1. **Prepare the Pastry:**
    - Roll out puff pastry and cut into squares. Place a spoonful of apricot jam in the center of each square. Fold into triangles or shapes of choice.
2. **Bake:**
    - Brush with egg wash and sprinkle with almonds. Bake at 375°F (190°C) for 15-18 minutes until golden.

Rustic Apple Galette

Ingredients:

- 1 premade pie crust
- 2 large apples, thinly sliced
- 2 tablespoons granulated sugar
- 1 tablespoon brown sugar
- 1/4 teaspoon cinnamon
- 1 tablespoon unsalted butter, cut into small pieces
- 1 egg (for egg wash)

Instructions:

1. **Assemble the Galette:**
   - Roll out pie crust onto parchment paper. Arrange apple slices in the center, leaving a 2-inch border. Sprinkle with sugar, brown sugar, and cinnamon. Dot with butter.
2. **Bake:**
   - Fold edges of the crust over the apples, pleating as needed. Brush with egg wash. Bake at 375°F (190°C) for 30-35 minutes until golden and bubbly.

www.ingramcontent.com/pod-product-compliance
Lightning Source LLC
LaVergne TN
LVHW081325060526
838201LV00055B/2466